Original title:

Under the Grow Light

Copyright © 2025 Creative Arts Management OÜ
All rights reserved.

Author: Clara Whitfield
ISBN HARDBACK: 978-1-80581-731-4
ISBN PAPERBACK: 978-1-80581-258-6
ISBN EBOOK: 978-1-80581-731-4

In the Radiant Embrace

In the glow, the plants sway,
Dancing leaves, what a display!
Talking to a tomato sprout,
"Hey, are you sure you're a stout?"

Cacti tell jokes, oh so sharp,
While ferns play tunes on a harp.
The basil dreams of pasta sauce,
While orchids debate sheer gloss.

Beneath the Sun's Whisper

A sunflower's tale begins to unfold,
"Did you hear the one about that marigold?"
The daisies giggle with glee,
"Let's prank the broccoli, just you and me!"

Chillies boast of spicy flair,
Radishes blush without a care.
The herbs gossip, oh what a spree,
"Did you know, thyme's not as funny as me?"

Nurtured by Luminescence

Little sprouts in their bright nest,
"Oh look, it's time for our growth fest!"
The lettuce wears shades, feeling cool,
"Why did the carrot leave the pool?"

Peppers play tag, zipping around,
Chasing shadows on the ground.
The snap peas giggle as they grow,
"Watch out for the slow-mo tomato show!"

A Dance of Shadows and Beams

In this light, the veggies glow,
"Shall we dance? Let's put on a show!"
The radish twirls, a vibrant spin,
While the kale mocks, "I'm the real win!"

Carrots and beets line up to prance,
Freestyle, jump, oh what a chance!
Together, they jive in this spot,
In a bountiful dance, they give it a shot!

The Warmth Between Leaves

In a room, plants giggle and sway,
Reaching for snacks on a sunny buffet.
Photosynthesis parties are all the rage,
Photosynthesizing on a leafy stage.

Brought two friends from the garden store,
One's a cactus, couldn't take it anymore.
Got sunburned and started to pout,
The others just laughed and danced about.

Illuminated Roots

Down below where it's dark and neat,
Roots are having their own little feast.
They nibble on nutrients, oh what a treat,
While shooting up, they don't miss a beat.

Said one root to another, "Let's dig deep!"
"I hear the compost has secrets to keep!"
With giggles and whispers, they delve and dive,
In this soil party, they feel alive.

Harvesting Dreams at Dusk

As the sun dips low, the veggies awake,
Carrots and radishes start to shake.
Plans for the future they start to share,
"Let's grow taller, no time to spare!"

With dreams of burgers and salads so bright,
They giggle at harvest, a culinary delight.
"Don't forget dressings, we want them zesty!"
Radishes flipped, "I'll be the bestie!"

Growing Towards the Light

Every sprout seeks a glow, what a sight,
They stretch their leaves towards the bright.
One cheeky plant yelled, "I'm on the run!"
"Catch me if you can, I'm having fun!"

A leafy race for the ultimate beam,
They trip on soil, but gasp, what a dream!
Jokingly swaying, they say with a cheer,
"Life's a greenhouse, let's bring on the beer!"

Light-Woven Gardens

In garden beds, the greens all sway,
Trying to dance, but they just delay.
Tomatoes giggle, peas are so sly,
Waving to bees as they buzz on by.

The carrots are doing a wiggly jig,
While radishes cheer, feeling quite big.
Herbs in a chorus, a fragrant delight,
Wishing the sun would stay out all night.

Growth's Gentle Mirage

In a world of dream where veggies conspire,
Cucumbers plot to grow ever higher.
Zucchinis wear hats, oh what a scene,
While peppers debate on who's the best green.

The lettuce is laughing, it's quite a hoot,
Puns from the squash, oh what a toot!
Each leaf a joke, each sprout a prank,
Living it up in their leafy prank bank.

The Alchemy of Light

More radiance, more fun, they all agree,
In the sun's warm glow, they feel so free.
But when it rains, they squeak and moan,
"Where's our spark? We feel so alone!"

The herbs whisper secrets, the dirt holds a tale,
Of wild adventures, of a worm and a snail.
They plot mischief, a green leafy spree,
If only the sun would join their jubilee!

Flourishing in Radiance

A merry band of veggies take stage,
Performing their antics, one heart-warming page.
The beets wear costumes of velvety red,
While broccoli boasts of the dreams in its head.

Sweet peas in pods share jokes from the vine,
"Why did the sprout cross the road? To dine!"
All in good spirit, with laughter and cheer,
Under bright beams, there's nothing to fear.

A Canvas of Verdure

In a patch of plastic and glow,
The greens start to strut and show.
Lettuce winks with a cheeky grin,
While radishes giggle, 'Let's begin!'

The tomatoes are plotting a dance,
'Throw in some salsa, let's take a chance!'
Peppers prance, bright in their hues,
Spreading laughter like morning dews.

Cucumbers stretch like they just got up,
In this plot, there's never a hiccup.
With every leaf, there's a joke in play,
A verdant comedy, day after day.

So join the fun, take a seat,
In this garden, life is sweet.
With humor sprouting from every seed,
Laughter and veggies are all we need.

Hydrogen Dreams

In a bubble of science and greenery,
Hydrogen dreams, oh, how they stir me.
Oxygen dances with carbon too,
A party of atoms, in moody hue.

Plants wear goggles, think they are cool,
Reciting the rules of the hydroponic school.
Lightbulbs wink like stars in the night,
As seedlings giggle, oh what a sight!

One sprout said, 'I dream of a tree,'
While others snickered, 'Just let us be!'
In the realm of roots and silly schemes,
Life's a laugh in these hydrogen dreams.

What's next for the crew in this space?
Perhaps a meeting to plan the next race.
With water and nutrients, they scheme and plot,
In hydrogen we trust, laugh a whole lot!

Songs of the Cultivated

In the rhythm of growth, hear the tune,
Cabbages croon to the light of the moon.
Radishes bop to a funky beat,
While kale takes a break, shakes its leafy feet.

The herbs are jamming, basil's in charge,
Sage hits the notes, while thyme goes large.
Mint brings the beat with a zesty flair,
In this garden concert, there's magic in the air.

With roots as their drums and soil for a stage,
The veggies perform, oh, but they age!
Lettuce bops as the tomatoes sway,
A cultivated symphony, brightening the day.

So grab your forks, join the crowd,
In this wacky garden, we sing out loud.
For every bite of laughter and cheer,
Is a song of the cultivated growing near!

Silent Sprouts

In the hush of the night, sprouts start to joke,
With tiny whispers, they're ready to poke.
'How tall will you be?' one leaf softly cried,
'As tall as a house!' the peas all replied.

The carrots chuckle from depths of the earth,
'We're the root crew, we're always in mirth!'
While beets roll over with a red-hued laugh,
'We'll find our way to the top, on our own path!'

With whispers of growth and laughter they spread,
As cucumber wishes for a comfy bed.
'Will we grow bigger over the weeks?'
They giggle and whisper in playful shrieks.

So here in the silence, with warmth all around,
Sprouts plot their fun on seedling ground.
In the quiet of night, they speak their own truths,
These silent sprouts share the joy of green youth.

Rhapsody in Green

In the corner, things sprout and bloom,
A cabbage tries to dance, making room.
Tomatoes chat about their rounder form,
While carrots gossip, finding their norm.

Each leaf has a tale, a joke to be told,
Basil claims to be the bravest and bold.
Pepper seeds chuckle, eager to shine,
As they plot their ascent, all perfectly fine.

The herbs form a band with pots as their stage,
Playing sweet tunes, setting the wage.
The radishes laugh, rolling with cheer,
In their leafy kingdom, they have no fear.

While sunlight's away, they light up their night,
With laughter and giggles, they feel so bright.
In this quirky garden, joy takes its place,
Where veggies unite, a comical space.

Cultivating Light

A potted plant sports shades like a star,
Sunglasses so cool, like it's going far.
Each leaf flips and flops like it's on a spree,
Shouting, 'Hey world, come grow along with me!'

The seedlings sing songs about soil so fine,
Claiming their roots in a pretty straight line.
They brag about water and sunshine galore,
Swapping their secrets, they'll grow even more.

With potting mix tossed like confetti in glee,
The veggies celebrate their cozy jubilee.
A cucumber winks, 'I've got the best lines!'
While broccoli flexes, 'Check out my designs!'

Their laughter resounds, a bubble of fun,
Each tiny sprout beams, 'Look what we've done!'
Under this glow, it's a riotous sight,
Cultivating joy, and sprouting delight.

Fruitful Luminance

Bananas in pajamas swing from their leaves,
Pineapples argue with plush, leafy thieves.
Strawberries brag with their sweet, juicy flair,
While lemons just pucker, caught in the glare.

The veggies plot mischief, a playful surprise,
Dressing up radishes as cute little spies.
As sunlight showers their vibrant parade,
Chillin' in green, their worries allayed.

Pumpkins compete to show who's the king,
With squash making jokes, oh the laughter they bring!
The mist creeps in, a party set right,
Every fruit and veggie dancing with delight.

With all of this fun, who needs the sun?
A disco of plants, celebrating as one.
In this fruity realm, under bright beams,
Laughter and joy sprout, fulfilling our dreams.

A Symphony of Sprouts

Let's gather the sprouts for a grand serenade,
With carrots and cucumbers, they're all well-played.
The greens strum their leaves, a rustling tune,
While radishes roll, sharing jokes 'neath the moon.

Tomatoes compose with a squishy delight,
Whispering secrets of growth through the night.
Their vines twist and twirl in extravagant flair,
Each trying to outshine the other laid bare.

Together, they dance in a botanical rave,
With laughter and joy, they boldly behave.
Beans climb the trellis, seeking the sound,
While peas gather round, making circles quite round.

In this leafy concert, the veggies unite,
Creating a show, oh what a sight!
Under the brilliance of their world so spry,
They sprout with laughter, reaching for the sky.

Wind Beneath the Leaves

In a garden where plants wiggle,
They dance, they sway, oh what a giggle.
Sunlight tickles when it shines,
Leaves start laughing, doing fine lines.

The carrots joke, with roots so deep,
'We're the veg that never sleep!'
Tomatoes blushing, oh so red,
'Look at us, we're well-bred!'

The daisies wink, with petals wide,
Flowers boastful, full of pride.
With wind beneath, they start to play,
In their leafy world, they sway all day.

The herbs join in, with scents so sweet,
'We spice things up, can't be beat!'
Garden shenanigans galore,
In this green paradise, who could ask for more?

Lush Horizons

In a world where greens are bright,
Giggles bubble in pure delight.
Potatoes talk, they dig their own,
'We're the roots that have outgrown!'

Cucumbers stretch, long and lean,
'We're the coolest ones you've seen!'
Peppers puff up with a grin,
'Spice us up, let fun begin!'

Even weeds joke, getting bold,
'We're the plants you never told!'
They wiggle in the breeze, so spry,
Making all the veggies sigh.

Lush horizons full of cheer,
Each plant whispers, "Stay right here!"
From tiny sprouts to those that climb,
Nature's laughter is simply sublime.

The Light's Gentle Embrace

Glow from the bulb, so warm and bright,
Plants gather round, it's quite a sight.
They tell tall tales about the day,
In their leafy land, they often play.

A sunflower giggles, tall and proud,
'Watch me dance, I attract a crowd!'
Beans are laughing with a twist,
'We climb so high, you can't resist!'

The greens whisper secrets, soft and low,
'We outshine the rest, don't you know?'
In this warmth, they sway and smile,
Growing together, style by style.

And when the night begins to creep,
They'll dream of sunshine, not a peep.
In their cozy place, they feel the grace,
Of the gentle glow, their warm embrace.

Flourishing in the Glow

In a cozy nook, the greens all meet,
They're telling tales, oh what a treat!
With roots so deep, they stomp and shout,
'Join the party, let's dance it out!'

Little shoots peek, just breaking ground,
'We're the sprouts, joy knows no bound!'
In hues of green, they're full of cheer,
Growing together, year after year.

Radishes rave, with a rosy hue,
'We're spicy and crispy, check us too!'
Lettuce laughs, as it takes a bow,
With leafy antics, they steal the show.

In this garden, under the gleam,
They flourish together, a jolly team.
With nature's humor, they're bound to grow,
In their funny little world, oh what a glow!

The Bright Side of Growth

I tell my plants a funny joke,
They laugh by yawning, what a poke!
In this warm glow, they stretch so tall,
Who knew light could make them laugh at all?

With every leaf, they dance and sway,
Under false stars, they play all day.
Like tiny comedians in minted green,
Their punchlines drip with chlorophyll sheen.

When I water, they splutter and sneeze,
A nature's comedy, if you please!
Potting soil does a jig now and then,
Making up for the lack of decent men.

So here's to the laughter, the fun and cheer,
In this lively patch, there's nothing to fear.
As I nurture with joy, they do the same,
In this bright world, we're all in the game.

Touch of the Artificial Sun

Oh, the glow in my room is quite divine,
Plants believe it's their disco time!
Photosynthesis waltzing across the floor,
With every turn, they're begging for more.

Dancing ferns with elegant flair,
While the cacti just don't seem to care.
The herbs gossip in whispers so low,
'Did you see the begonia? Stealing the show!'

Grow lights buzzing like a busy bee,
A symphony played in green harmony.
But when the sun dims, the jokes get bleak,
Plants plotting a prank – oh, what a peak!

Yet every dawn brings a silly surprise,
Like a tomato in shades, under sunny skies.
These tales of mirth keep my heart so young,
In this frolicsome garden, I stay among.

Flora's Electric Dream

In a world lit up, the flowers conspire,
With giggles and laughter, they reach higher.
Through zappy dreams and leafy quirks,
In this electric glow, no one jerks!

The basil winks, the thyme rolls its eyes,
While succulents bask, oh what a prize!
This bright insanity, a circus it seems,
Each petal a player in botanical dreams.

At midnight they plot for the moonlight dance,
Arguing over who gets the last chance.
"Step back, my friend, or risk garden strife!"
They jostle, knock pots, what a plantful life!

With every green friend, the fun won't cease,
This laugh-filled garden, a haven of peace.
When day breaks again, joy's still in stream,
In Flora's delightfully strange electric dream.

Haven of Luminous Growth

In the cozy corner, plants burst with glee,
Cracking jokes, both tall and wee.
Dandelions chuckle, wise old trees grin,
While the marigolds cheer for the fab win.

"Look at me, a leafy superstar!"
A zinnia boasts from its shining jar.
Even the soil knows how to play,
Whispering secrets from the compost bay.

At times they plan a takeover feat,
Flamboyant ferns bring the ultimate heat!
In this brightness, non-stop hilarity reigns,
As they cultivate jokes along with gains.

Amidst the light, they'll forever bloom,
Living in laughter—there's always room.
From sprout to bloom, their spirits so bright,
In this haven of growth, it's pure delight!

Reviving Roots

Beneath the glow, they stretch and sway,
With leafy whispers, they laugh and play.
'Is it bath time or just some sun?'
They wiggle their roots, just for fun.

Some dance like they're at a wild rave,
While others compost, feeling quite brave.
'I swear, I saw a tomato do a jig,'
Even the carrots are pulling a gig.

A Spectrum of Flourish

A spectrum shines with shades of delight,
In this garden, everyone's quite bright.
The chives wear shades, feeling so cool,
While daisies gossip by the watering pool.

The peppers are primping, such colors they flaunt,
'To be juicy and spicy is what we want.'
As broccoli breaks into a dance-off spree,
'We're the coolest veggies, can't you see?'

Chasing the Dimming

When the light dims low, they start to frown,
'Come back, oh rays, don't let us drown!'
The ferns wave their fronds, trying to cheer,
'It's just a shadow, so have no fear!'

The tomatoes pout, feeling quite smug,
'We'd shine like stars, if not for the bug!'
Yet even in gloom, they find a way,
'Sori not to shine, but we'll still slay!'

The Embrace of Brightness

In the warm embrace of radiant beams,
Every plant stirs awake from their dreams.
'Up and at 'em, let's stretch and grin!'
They giggle and bounce, ready to begin.

The sunflowers stand tall, striking a pose,
While mint makes a splash, perfuming the close.
'Is it party time? Let's have a blast!'
In this vibrant scene, they're having a blast.

Glimmers of Potential

In pots they sit, a leafy crew,
Dreaming of skies and morning dew.
With goofy smiles, they stretch and sway,
Hoping to sprout and dance all day.

"Oh look at me!" the basil cries,
"I'm a superstar in disguise!"
While sage just laughs, "I'm wise, you see,
But make sure not to overwater me!"

A tomato blushes, ripe and round,
"I'm destined to be the best in town!"
With every droplet, each little cheer,
They sprout ambitions, year after year.

So here's to growth, with laughter bright,
In pots apart, but hearts delight.
Together they'll flourish, that's the plan,
Funny little plants, a garden band!

Sun-Kissed Secrets

Peeking leaves, so soft and green,
Whispering secrets, what could they mean?
With sunbeams tickling every stem,
They plot a party, oh what a gem!

"Let's play tag!" the mint leaves shout,
While thyme's too busy spinning about.
Catching rays like it's a game,
Throwing shadows, never the same.

Dancing petals flutter with glee,
As root systems form a symphony.
"I grow taller!" one sweet pepper glees,
But the rest just chuckle, "You'll trip on these!"

In this wild jungle of joy and cheer,
Every sprout's got a tale to share here.
With sun-kissed laughter, they thrive and glow,
A whimsical garden, putting on a show!

Tending to the Light Within

In a cozy nook, they tend their dreams,
Roots entwined, or so it seems.
With every drop of water splashed,
They giggle and wiggle, a colorful bash.

"Oh me, oh my!" the radish sings,
"Ready to bloom, let's see what spring brings!"
While chard shimmies, all decked in flair,
Each little leaf with time to spare.

As they stretch upward, reaching for glee,
"I'll win the height contest!" yells the pea.
Then rosemary hops, "But I smell divine!"
A competition, oh so fine!

United they flourish, each story unfolds,
Life in the garden, a joy to behold.
With laughter and growth, they share their delight,
Tending to dreams, in the soft, warm light!

Illuminated Whispers

Beneath the bulb, they gather tonight,
Sharing their secrets, oh what a sight!
"Why did the tomato cross the plot?"
"To ketchup with friends, oh what a thought!"

Chives giggle softly, teasing the thyme,
"Dare to dance? You'll be sublime!"
With each little flicker, they light up the lore,
Each word is a spark, who could ask for more?

The sunflower beams, "I'm king of this space!"
But all the others shout, "Give us a trace!"
Flashes of joy, as laughter ensues,
In this bright haven, they banter and muse.

Illuminated whispers, wild and free,
In the kingdom of sprouts, where all can agree.
Every green soul finds its chance to play,
Together they shine, come what may!

A Garden of Electric Hues

In a plot where veggies dance,
A disco ball, not chance!
Tomatoes flaunt their green attire,
While peppers twirl, a bright conspire.

Radishes blush, shy, but bold,
Waving roots, if truth be told.
Cucumbers giggle, bounce with glee,
In this garden jubilee!

Bees in sunglasses zoom about,
Pollinating with a shout!
Dancing daisies sway and spin,
In this space, we all win!

Even carrots dream of fame,
With veggie celebs, who's to blame?
Here we laugh and sprout with cheer,
In this garden, fun is near!

Cradled in Celestial Rays

Within beams that tickle leaves,
Nature's mischief never deceives.
Squash plays hide and seek with sun,
While cabbages make silly puns.

A flower winks, says 'Look at me!'
While broccoli sips on herbal tea.
Zucchini's trying out a hat,
It's quite the sight, imagine that!

Beans chat gossip, sweet and sour,
Swaying with all their veggie power.
Radical radishes plot and scheme,
Chasing after that wild dream.

Oh, what joy, this playful scene,
With fruits and veggies, all so keen.
Laughter echoes in the air,
It's a cosmic garden affair!

Growth in the Gentle Gleam

In a nook where plants conspire,
Leaves are glistening, rise and aspire.
Sprouts poke heads, curious and bright,
Excited for their evening light.

A spinach patch makes jokes galore,
While onions giggle, rolling on the floor.
Peas are apt to sing a tune,
While carrots dream of a cartoon.

Treetops wave, sharing virtuous tales,
In this place, even soil prevails.
Each seedling shines with joy in glee,
Proclaiming, 'Come join our jubilee!'

Growth in the gleam is never glum,
As laughter fills the air, here we come!
In this plot of whimsy and light,
We harvest joy and pure delight!

Threads of Radiance

Threads twine through each leafy scene,
Crafting laughter, pure and keen.
Petunias giggle, swaying low,
While thyme tosses a witty flow.

Cucumbers smile, full of jest,
In this patch, we are truly blessed.
Basil spins and twirls so free,
Dancing in a leafy spree.

Peppers pirouette, full of spice,
Zestful blooms, oh so nice!
Spinach witches cast a spell,
In this plot, all's well, we dwell!

Harvesting humor in the sun,
With nature's fun, we're never done.
Threads of radiance fill the day,
Join the dance, come out and play!

Cherishing the Brightest Moments

In a room where veggies chatter,
Little sprouts sing, 'What's the matter?'
Dancing leaves, oh what a sight,
Chasing beams with sheer delight.

Basil's gossip, cilantro's glee,
Tomato dreams of being free.
Sunshine giggles from afar,
While broccoli dreams of being a star.

Radishes hide in playful shrouds,
As peas poke fun at passing clouds.
They share their jokes, a witty crew,
With every pun, they grow anew.

So here's to joy in every leaf,
In happy greens, let's find belief.
For every beam that kisses earth,
We cherish all this silly mirth.

In the Embrace of Radiance

Glow-worms in the garden plot,
Whisper secrets, oh so hot.
Eager sprouts, they wiggle and sway,
Love the warmth, but shy away.

Tomatoes blush at the spotlight,
While radishes yell, 'This is our night!'
Lettuce laughs at tall ambition,
Planted dreams in bright rendition.

Cucumber thrones, they wear with pride,
In green attire, they can't hide.
While peppers jest in shades so bold,
Their funny tales, a joy to behold.

With humor flying on wings of light,
These little plants take flight at night.
In the glow, they play and preen,
In every corner, a whimsical scene.

Beneath the Neon Glow

In a corner, all spruced up,
The quirky greens fill every cup.
Microgreens in a funky spree,
They giggle hard, 'Wanna join me?'

Carrots wear shades, look quite cool,
Dreaming of summers in a pool.
While eggplants joke about their hue,
In the bright, they dance, oh so true.

Herbs recite their cheeky lines,
Basil winks at the sunny vines.
Pepper shouts, 'Watch my show!',
As they bask in the neon glow.

And in the merry, vibrant scene,
All the plants are full of keen.
With snapshots of laughter overhead,
A harvest of mirth, and joy widespread.

Harvesting Shadows

In the twilight, shadows play,
Plants recount their funny day.
On tiny stems, big dreams reside,
Chasing giggles, they can't hide.

Cabbage swings in leafy skirts,
Lettuce jokes about its quirks.
As beets blush deeper than before,
Corn laughs, 'Never a boring chore!'

Silly herbs, they crack wise jokes,
Parsnips laugh, while thyme provokes.
All join in, a jovial feast,
In playful spirits, they are pleased.

So let's raise a toast, from above,
To leafy greens and all their love.
In shadows deep and whispers low,
We harvest laughter, let it grow.

Secrets in the Spectrum

When I water my plants, they giggle with glee,
They whisper their secrets, just between me.
In hues of green, red, and a touch of blue,
They dance in the light, oh, if only you knew.

The tomatoes tell jokes while the beans play charades,
While the carrots recite their proud escapades.
The cilantro just sighs, it's too cool for this game,
But its fragrance brings laughter, what's wrong with its name?

Peppers wear sun hats, they're quite in their prime,
While the basil's practicing for its stand-up time.
So I sit with my sprouts, in this vibrant brigade,
In the spectrum's glow, my worries all fade.

When night falls around, they turn off their smiles,
And sleep in the glow, dreaming brightly for miles.
But tomorrow will come, as it always has done,
With secrets on leaves, let the growing be fun!

Green Dreams in the Glow

In a cozy old corner where sunlight does play,
My leaves dream in colors of vibrant display.
They chatter and gossip, all in a hush,
While I sip my tea and watch them all blush.

The spinach claims bravado, the lettuce takes bets,
On who'll sprout the fastest, no regrets or debts.
The herbs are all laughing, it's a wild little circus,
With parsley as ringmaster, quite eager to serve us.

The cacti roll eyes, they're just prickly skeptics,
"As if we'd join this riot of green and perspective!"
But the daisies all nod, looking fab in their spots,
Saying, "Join the fun party, we're all green with thoughts!"

So I settle in, wrapped in my leafy brigade,
Sipping dreams from a cup, by the glow I've made,
A wild world of laughter, where sunshine will flow,
In this ridiculous garden, where green dreams all grow!

Photosynthesis of the Soul

Oh, to bask in the glow, like a plant in delight,
Where photons come dancing, on a silent night.
My soul thirsts for laughter, as I lean toward the beam,
Transforming my worries into a joyful dream.

Photosynthesis whispers, "Just chill for a while,"
"Live green, laugh hard, and wear a big smile."
The daisies agree, with a sway and a spin,
"Life's too short for gloom, let's let the fun in!"

As sunlight trickles down, it tickles my heart,
Making silly shadows that wiggle and dart.
The grapevines are gossiping, full of sweet blooms,
Each leaf tells a secret, banishing glooms.

Together we flourish, in this vibrant light show,
Where each tiny sprout is a star in a row.
So cheers to the glow, and to laughter that rolls,
In the great photosynthesis of our souls!

Cultivating Hope's Bright Flame

In pots of pure wonder, where dreams seem to sprout,
I'm nurturing laughter, with a hint of a pout.
Each seed is a giggle, each sprout is a cheer,
Growing bright in the light, my worries are mere.

With shovels of joy, we dig deep into play,
Planting seeds of tomorrow in a quirky bouquet.
The sunflowers stand tall, with their heads held so proud,
While the thyme and the mint form a curious crowd.

The broccoli bustles with 'fit for a king,'
While kale cracks a joke about fitness and bling.
I swear I can hear them, in chortles they croon,
"Let's cultivate hope while we dance to the moon!"

As twilight arrives, laughter lingers so bright,
In this garden of whimsy, where each leaf feels right.
So here's to our dreams, and the joy that they tame,
We're cultivating futures, with hope's bright flame!

Blossoms of the Artificial Sun

In a room where plants all grin,
They stretch their leaves, where to begin?
With neon rays, they play the part,
A circus show, a leafy art.

The cacti dance with nimble feet,
They twirl and twist, what a treat!
While ferns wiggle in delight,
As fake sunshine fills the night.

Their colors pop, a lively spree,
In this odd greenhouse jubilee.
A chlorophyll fiesta grows,
With silly seeds that strike a pose.

So here's to plants, the funny sort,
In this bright room, they cavort!
With laughter tossed from leaf to leaf,
Join the fun, and toss your grief!

Warmth of the Orb

In a corner glows an orb so bright,
Shining boldly through the night.
The fern insists it's beach day,
While succulents laugh and sway.

The petunias wear their best shades,
Underneath this glow, they parade.
While orchids sip on faux sun tea,
This wild party's just for me!

A lumpy squash throws a grand ball,
With wiggly roots, we'll have a ball!
Basil spins with a fragrant flair,
In artificial sunlight, we dare!

So gather 'round, o' leafy friends,
This funny warmth just never ends.
With roots that tickle and laughter to sow,
Let's dance and bloom, let's steal the show!

Photosynthetic Ballet

The greenery reads a ballet guide,
With pirouettes, they take great pride.
A leafy troupe, they leap and twirl,
In this bizarre, green wonder world.

The lilies stretch, then take a bow,
While broccoli shows off its wow!
With rhythmic waves, they sway around,
A colorful show without a sound.

Oh, how the spinach flips and flies,
Underneath those glowing skies.
With sunlight's humor, they delight,
In this strange garden of delight.

So grab a seat, enjoy the show,
A leafy ballet, a funny flow.
Who knew that greens could dance so free?
Join the laughter, it's where we should be!

Aurora of Green

A radiant glow fills the air,
Plants gather 'round, they just don't care.
In this bright hue, they chirp and sing,
Bringing joy, it's a leafy fling!

Kale cracks jokes, what a wise guy,
While beets blush deep, oh my, oh my!
Each herb adds spice to the fun,
In this madcap show, we've just begun!

The vines climb high to catch the light,
They climb and tumble, what a sight!
The tomatoes roll with laughter's zeal,
Creating giggles a veggie can feel.

Oh, what a scene, this colorful spree,
A green aurora, wild and free!
With happiness sprouting out of the dirt,
Join the chuckles; let's all convert!

Growth Beneath the Stream

In a pot by the sink, my plants all cheer,
They sip at the water, oh so sincere.
With a wink and a nod, they stretch out their leaves,
I swear they're plotting all sorts of pranks and thieves.

The basil does pirouettes, the thyme does a jig,
The parsley's the bouncer, all tiny yet big.
They gossip of sunlight, the phantom they chase,
While dreaming of sunlight, a bright, fuzzy place.

Each morning I find them in wild, silly states,
Doing yoga and aerobics, oh how time awaits!
The lettuce is laughing, the mint's in a spin,
I sometimes think my plants might just grow a grin.

In the night, they conspire, crafting their schemes,
Oh, the leafy antics of these verdant dreams.
They dance through the soil, embracing the glance,
Of a curious gardener who joins in their dance.

When Shadows Bloom

Beneath the shelves where shadows blend,
Plants giggle softly, their leafy trend.
The ferns tell tales of colossal heights,
While beans engage in their aerial flights.

A cactus claims, with a prickly sigh,
"I'm the strongest here, won't you even try?"
The moss keeps giggling, in a fuzzy coat,
Saying, "What's all this fuss? Do you want some toast?"

In the corner pot, a rogue spider plant,
Hums a silly tune with a verdant chant.
"I bloom in the dark, against all the odds,
With a wink and a smile, I befuddle the gods!"

Oh, how they flourish in their shadowed room,
Bringing joy and laughter, dispelling the gloom.
Each twist and each turn, they charge up the air,
When shadows bloom, it's a joyful affair!

Hues of the Verdant Heart

In pots of green with a splash of red,
A kaleidoscope boasts of the mischief they've spread.
The peas do a jig while the chives like to hum,
Shouting, "Who needs sunlight? We're already fun!"

With a sprinkle of water, a dash of a cheer,
These quirky greens whisper, "We have no fear!"
The carrots underground play their hide-and-seek,
While radishes chuckle, their colors so chic.

They talk of secrets that only they know,
In the rhythm of growing, they put on a show.
A leaf from the basil plots against the thyme,
In the culinary kingdom, it's truly prime time.

As colors mix wildly in their playful dance,
It's a riot of hues that gives life a chance.
In this lively spot, where green hearts ignite,
Each shade tells a story, it's all pure delight!

Basking in Luminescence

In a room where the glow meets the leafy surprise,
Plants lounge like beachgoers beneath sunny skies.
The succulents giggle with their sandcastle dreams,
While the violets snicker, or so it seems.

Each glow is a tickle to their tiny greens,
Causing leafy laughter, with all of their schemes.
Ferns are planning parties, the aloe brings cake,
Saying, "Join us for snacks, for goodness' sake!"

Beeswax candles flicker while herbs start to sway,
Claiming, "Dance with us for a bright, happy day!"
The spinach just chuckles, saying, "Look at me!
I'm the life of the garden! Come dance and be free!"

So here in this haven, where plants love to play,
In a glow that encourages their vibrant ballet.
They bask in the lumens, their antics unfurl,
In a world of green laughter, a humorous twirl!

The Glow of New Beginnings

In the corner, plants do sway,
With tiny leaves, they dance and play.
They stretch so high, oh look at them,
In search of sun, like tiny gems.

A sprout sneezes, who knew they could?
A leaf proclaims, "I feel so good!"
They giggle, tease each growing stem,
In this bright room, they're all a gem.

The water sings, the soil grins,
Each little herb, a world of wins.
They wink at me, as if to say,
"Let's grow and play the whole day away!"

With every pulse of vibrant light,
They twirl and spin, a silly sight.
Though rooted firm, they still can jive,
In this bright glow, they feel alive!

Bright Horizons in Darkness

A leaf peeks out from its dark bed,
Stretching out far, it's filled with dread.
"Where's the sun?" it loudly cries,
"Brighten my day with golden skies!"

A tiny sprout, with all its might,
Said, "I'll grow tall; I'll reach the height!"
With laughter rich, it climbs the wall,
"Watch out, world, I'm having a ball!"

In this odd space of gleaming cheer,
Plants chat about the light they steer.
"Did you know?" one says with glee,
"Photosynthesis is the key!"

So here we chuckle, root and vine,
As buds and blooms in rhythm rhyme.
Embracing whims, we take our stands,
In our bright world, we form tight bands.

Nature's Luminous Symphony

A glowworm sings, or is that a sprout?
In leafy tunes, they twist about.
With sunshine dreams, they serenade,
This is how the green parade!

The ferns flap arms, like jazzing fools,
Dancing to nature's shiny rules.
Sassy petals strut their stuff,
With roots so deep, they can't get enough.

"Hey there, bloom! You shine so bright!"
Said the shy green thing, filled with fright.
"Don't worry friend, just take the chance,
Join us now, let's all dance!"

Together they hum, a giggly tune,
With squiggly stems, they join the swoon.
A symphony of joy and cheer,
In this bright place, nothing's unclear!

The Warm Touch of Creation

With a flick of light, they come alive,
In silly sprigs, they thrive and jive.
The tender warmth, it makes them glow,
In this joyful show, their colors flow.

"Oh look at me!" cries the pumpkin sprout,
With a wiggly dance, it shouts out loud.
"Bet you can't reach!" says the leafy sage,
In this bright realm, they engage!

The soil giggles, tickles their toes,
As roots hold on, that's how it goes.
With cozy hugs of warmth and light,
They smile, they peek, it's such a sight!

Each day's a party in this merry room,
As they unfold and steadily bloom.
With mismatched leaves, they laugh and sway,
In this wonderland, we'll laugh and play!

Greenhouse Reverie

In the corner, a tomato grins,
While a pepper dances, oh what a spin!
Lettuce whispers secrets so sly,
As carrots wish they could touch the sky.

Cacti complain, 'Why's it so bright?'
While daisies gossip about the night.
Herbs are plotting a spicy caper,
While radishes dream of a papered taper.

Ferns are flexing, feeling quite bold,
In their leafy coats of emerald gold.
Petunias giggle at all the fuss,
While gardeners chat about why they must!

Yet through the chaos, blooms can't resist,
For every sprout knows they exist,
To bring a chuckle, a joyful scene,
In this whimsical world, oh so green!

Radiance of Renewal

Beets wear sunglasses, feeling so cool,
While the squash declare, 'We're the growth rule!'
A sunflower boasts, 'I'm the tallest here,'
While peas make jokes, full of cheer.

The potted palms dance in the air,
While tiny sprouts joke, 'Do we have a prayer?'
With vines that wiggle and leaves that sway,
It's a party of plants, come what may!

Tomatos set up a comedy show,
With jokes only they really know.
Carrots in caps, looking quite proud,
Join in the laughter, drawing a crowd.

Chives keep whispering plant puns of old,
While marigolds flaunt their petals of gold.
What a spectacle, a garden so bright,
Where humor blooms in every daylight!

In the Luminous Haven

In a bright nook, where the green things grow,
A parsley takes selfies, striking a pose.
A basil cheekily winks with a grin,
While celery dreams of a marathon win.

The radishes scream, 'We're the root of the jest!'
While mushrooms throw shade, feeling quite blessed.
Foliage flips like it's dance party night,
With foliage twirls and roots taking flight.

Tomatoes throw caution and catch falling light,
Exchanging their jokes in the glow of the night.
Onions chuckle, 'Don't peel if you can!'
It's a lighthearted hoedown, that's the plan!

They trade their fun tales, make bright plans anew,
As bulbs sparkle brightly, beneath skies so blue.
With laughter and joy, this place knows no end,
In the glow where the veggies and jokes all blend!

Nurtured by Artifice

Beneath the glow, where the sprouts take flight,
Tomatoes are telling their jokes every night.
Peppers keep scribbling their memoirs for fun,
While corn watches closely, 'Look, I'm the one!'

Herbs are debating who smells the best,
With mint making fun of the thyme's little test.
Radishes blush, full of glee and delight,
As broccoli chuckles, 'That's wrong, not right!'

Cucumbers stress over fashion trends,
In their leafy attire, they make amends.
Carrots and beets toss their shade at the sun,
Claiming they're the reason for all this fun!

As laughter erupts from the pots all around,
In this playful jungle, joy knows no bound.
A symphony of veggies, vibrant and bright,
Creating a world that's purely out of sight!

Tending to Light's Kiss

My plants are all prepped, dressed to the nines,
With shades of green and leaves like designs.
They wiggle and dance in their plastic abode,
While I'm just a gardener with a lighter load.

The broccoli's gossip, the tomatoes all laugh,
In their sunny spot, they're the chosen half.
"More light!" they shout, "We're ready to glow!"
"Just keep us away from that neighbor's crow!"

They stretch and they bend, striking a pose,
As if in a show with some twisty toes.
"Take a selfie!" they plead, so I give it a try,
But they're just too leafy; I can't say goodbye!

So here we all are, a motley crew,
With succulents jealous of the lettuce too.
They're heated and happy, with color abound,
In this weird little world where plants are profound.

In Petals of Artificial Dawn

Awake in the morning, my flora so bright,
Claiming each corner, they're basking in light.
I hum them a tune, and they nod with delight,
In this jungle of plastics, oh what a sight!

The cacti complain they've got prickles to spare,
While ferns with their fronds put on quite a flair.
"Stop hogging the light!" yells a poor little sprout,
While leafy divas strut, showing their clout.

I tiptoe around, avoiding the mess,
With watering cans, and my gardening dress.
The daisies decide to throw a wild bash,
But I just roll my eyes and watch them all crash.

The sun's not a threat here, just a soft glow,
Guiding my plants in this cosmic show.
I grumble and giggle, they're all my best pals,
In the shimmer of dawn, my botanical gals.

Glowing Canopy

In my little patch, there's a glowing spree,
Where snapshots of green play peek-a-boo with me.
The daisies are dancing, the basil's in tune,
While the herbs just critique, "That's not how you prune!"

Good vibes all around, giggles planted with care,
"More water!" they chant, "We'll shoot for the air!"
A potted romance blooms by the nearby wall,
As a cactus serenades – oh, who will take the fall?

The lettuce tells stories of salad days past,
While I snicker, "You've gotta grow fast!"
In this canopy's hug, life's an endless swirl,
Who knew gardening could get so absurd?

So here we all garden, in wires and light,
With jokes sprouting from each tender shoot, quite.
Let the laughter unfold, the plants have a blast,
In my glowing paradise, these moments are vast.

Botanical Luminescence

Green thumbs up! It's a party tonight,
With sprouts and their friends feeling quite alright.
Lettuce leads the cha-cha, and kale does the twist,
While herbs throw shade, watch them swing like a fist.

Flickering bulbs cast shadows of fun,
As ferns whisper secrets 'til the day is done.
"More light!" cries a sunflower, a diva so bold,
"Without me, this garden is terribly cold!"

The pepper plants blush as the carrots take charge,
Debating their size, who is growing large?
And though I might grumble, they brighten my day,
In this silly little world, plants dance, come what may.

As the cosmos turns, I watch them all thrive,
These quirky green pals, oh, how they arrive!
With petals and laughter, let's share in the glee,
For in this bright haven, it's just them and me.

The Celestial Germination

In a corner near the wall,
Little seeds do have a ball.
They wiggle, giggle, sprout with glee,
Waiting for their chance to be.

They wear their hats, the sun's delight,
Dancing under what feels right.
Water thinks it's on a spree,
Join the party, can you see?

Roots do tango, leaves take flight,
What a sight, it's pure delight!
A broccoli is in the mix,
Joking with a load of tricks.

Nature's stage, a vibrant show,
A leafy laugh, a green hi-ho!
Sprouting joy from tiny seeds,
Who knew they had such funny needs?

Awakening the Dormant

Deep in slumber, they do rest,
Seeds dreaming, oh, how they jest!
Toss and turn, awake they shout,
The world outside is what it's about.

With a nudge, the soil says, 'Go!'
Sunlight tickles, 'Time to grow!'
They stretch their limbs, so fresh and bright,
With a grumble, 'We're up, alright!'

A pea pod boasts of its green robe,
'Check me out,' it starts to probe.
Sprouts from carrots know they're cool,
Throw a dance party—nature's rule!

Friends in dirt, they break the mold,
Sharing stories, brave and bold.
Who knew dormancy was such a ride?
Awakened crew, now filled with pride!

Lush Echoes

In leafy chambers, whispers grow,
Echoing laughs, a soft hello.
A sprig of thyme tells jokes so fine,
While sage gives winks, just divine.

The basil band strums tunes so sweet,
While minty freshness takes a seat.
They twirl and sway in sunny cheer,
Filling the air with joy and jeer.

Sunlight's rays, a spotlight bright,
Foliage dances, pure delight.
Roots are tapping, saying, 'Yo!
Join our jam—come on, let's go!'

A party formed from twists and turns,
In laughter's warmth, the garden burns.
Nature's crew, forever tight,
In vibrant glee, they take to flight!

Dance of the Chloroplasts

Tiny green, the dancers spin,
Chloroplasts chuckle, 'Let's begin!'
They groove to rhythms of daylight,
Turn sunlight into pure delight.

Photosynthesis, their funky beat,
With every twist, they feel the heat.
'Watch us shine!' the cells proclaim,
'We may be small, but play the game!'

A disco party, green and bright,
Swaying strands in the golden light.
They serve up sugar, what a treat,
'Dance with us, it cannot be beat!'

Life's a jive, with roots and feuilles,
Nature's revelry, a joy that fuels.
Join the dance, with leaves that sway,
In chlorophyll we find our play!

Illuminated Buds

In a room of glow, they sway and dance,
Little green buds, caught in a trance.
They wiggle and giggle, oh what a sight,
Taking selfies, basking in light.

Marijuana fiascos, oh what a game,
Telling each other, 'I'm not to blame!'
Photosynthesis parties, all night long,
With chlorophyll beats, they sing their song.

Some wear shades, thinking they're cool,
While others do yoga, following the 'rule.'
Rubbing leaves together, creating a sound,
In this leafy haven, joy abounds.

They dream of sunshine, warmth, and rain,
Sharing their hopes like a wild campaign.
With roots like gossipers, they spread out wide,
In their illuminated world, they take great pride.

The Sanctuary of Growth

In a cozy corner, all snug and bright,
Little sprouts gather, full of delight.
They pop and fizz like a bubbly drink,
With each glowing moment, they start to think.

From tiny seeds to leafy smiles,
Their awkward charm goes on for miles.
Playing hide and seek, they stretch and bend,
In this giggly garden, fun won't end.

A mossy carpet, it's quite the show,
As they swap their jokes, putting on a glow.
"Who needs the sun?" one boldly claims,
"I'm the star here, I'll win the games!"

With roots all tangled, they throw a ball,
Laughing together in that verdant hall.
As the day fades, they cozy up tight,
In this sanctuary, everything feels right.

Sheltered by Brightness

Under a canopy of shimmering rays,
Little leafy folks brighten their days.
With their painted petals, they strut around,
Creating a haven where laughter is found.

They play dress-up in vibrant attire,
Mixing up colors, they never tire.
Spreading gossip as they bask in cheer,
"Did you hear what that fern said? Oh dear!"

With water droplets as their shiny crowns,
They challenge each other to the funniest clowns.
In this bright-lit comedy, they bloom and twirl,
Life's much more fun with a green leafy whirl.

At night they gather, telling tales of glory,
Of sunny days and their leafy story.
In their sheltered world, they frolic and shine,
Making memories, growing fine.

Verdant Illumination

In the glow of magic, they sprout with glee,
Swaying in rhythm, wild and free.
They sprinkle laughter, like glittery dew,
Hoping their rivals will join in too.

Each leaf a joker, with stories to tell,
They chuckle and bubble, all under the spell.
"Here comes the gardener!" one whispers in jest,
"Quick! Strike a pose; it's time to impress!"

In a race for light, they stretch and they bend,
Roots tangled together, a leafy trend.
With each squabbly dance, they lift the mood,
In their vibrant kingdom, the fun's never crude.

So raise a glass, made of pure sunshine,
Cheers to the crew, feeling just divine.
Growing together, through thick and thin,
In this verdant world, let the laughter begin!

Pure Essence of Chlorophyll

In the corner of the room, they sway,
Dancing plants that love to play.
Photosynthesis in full swing,
Green dreams grow, like they're a king.

Neighbors peek with curious eyes,
"What's that glow? Is it a prize?"
I just chuckle, sip my tea,
These leafy pals are all with me.

Their laughter fills the humid space,
With each sprout, I find more grace.
Poking fun at sunlight's game,
Who knew plants could win at fame?

In this light, they bloom and thrive,
Wishing I could get that vibe!
Oh, to be a leaf, so carefree,
Wrapped in joy and jubilee.

Embraced by the Light

Waking early, plants are bright,
Sunshine trapped, oh what a sight!
They stretch and yawn in early morn,
Glow like stars, from night reborn.

"Look at us!" they whisper low,
"Best friends with beams, just watch us grow!"
With every ray, they giggle loud,
As if they're besting every crowd.

I swear I saw a leaf declare,
"Let's start a band, we've got the flair!"
With pots as drums and roots as strings,
Their funky beats would have no kings!

Oh, the laughter fills the air,
A garden party like a fair.
Swaying bodies, green and spry,
In this light, they'll always fly.

Elysium in Synthetic Rays

In a world where sunshine's shy,
They beam and glow, oh my, oh my!
"Turn up the dial, let's have some fun!"
Chlorophyll dreams, each day's a run.

"Who needs clouds? We'll shine so bright!"
Dancing leaves in the faux delight.
With eager roots, they seek the beat,
Electric vibes they can't defeat.

I jest and say, "What's your plan?"
"Max out the watts — we're the greenest fan!"
In laughter's glow, they seem to boast,
A jungle rave, oh what a toast!

When night falls down, and shadows creep,
They twinkle bright, even in sleep.
"Dream big, friends, there's more to swoon!"
Join the dance of the glowing moon.

Nature's Guiding Beacon

In this hodgepodge of glowing friends,
Each leaf a story that never ends.
"Need a guide? Just look this way!"
Illuminated in goofy play.

Among the fronds, a chatter spins,
"Who's the brightest? Let's begin!"
With each beam, they strut and cheer,
These spirited greens are loud and clear.

A wise old fern once said to me,
"Join our crew; it's leafy glee!"
Unruly sprouts with laughter loud,
A comedy show, a leafy crowd!

When friends swing over for a peek,
They gawk at greens that truly speak.
"Best light in town, that's plain to see!"
Together, we laugh, just plants and me.

From Seed to Light

In a pot where dreams reside,
A tiny sprout starts to confide.
It wiggles, it jiggles, a dance so fine,
"Grow up tall! You're destined to shine!"

The soil chuckles, a wise old friend,
"Hurry up, little one, don't just pretend!"
A worm gives a twist, says with a grin,
"You're in a race, let the fun begin!"

Sunbeams sparkle, a golden glee,
"Catch me if you can, come dance with me!"
The leaves wave back, they're feeling spry,
"Let's have a party, oh my, oh my!"

The gardener chuckles, with water in tow,
"Don't drink too fast, just take it slow.
It's not a marathon, it's just a spree,
So stretch those roots and be wild and free!"

Melodies of the Green Realm

In the garden, a chorus sings,
Petals flutter with the joy spring brings.
A ladybug leaps, then plays a tune,
"Let's rock this plot beneath the moon!"

The daisies sway, they toss and twirl,
While dandelions spin, they give a whirl.
"Watch out!" cries thyme, "here comes the breeze,
Try not to tumble, hold on with ease!"

A sunflower acts like the king of the show,
"Bow to my height, just look how I glow!"
While a sneaky little fern rolls its eyes,
"Your crown's just a wig, it's no big prize!"

The breeze whispers secrets, oh so sly,
"Hey there, plants, let out a sigh!
Let's dance together in this leafy scene,
The green realm's a stage for the fun machine!"

A Bright Garden Awakens

With the dawn, the garden wakes,
The veggies joke, "Let's bake some cakes!"
Zucchini giggles, cucumber grins,
"Who's got the frosting for our thin skins?"

The marigolds roll in their beds of gold,
"Let's have a toast, or maybe just hold!
We're the bright buds, the stars of the plot,
The sun's our spotlight, what a grand thought!"

The carrots are shy, buried deep in their dirt,
"Can we join in? We'll just wear a shirt!"
A beet blushes, says, "Don't be so coy,
Let the world see, you've got plenty of joy!"

The bees start to hum, a giggly refrain,
"Join the band, it's time to entertain!
We'll gather the nectar, bring sweetness about,
In this bright garden, we'll dance and shout!"

Revelations of Photosynthesis

In the lab of the leaves, a chef stirs away,
Mixing sunlight, a bright buffet.
"Add a pinch of air, a dash of rain,
Let's cook up some food, that's our domain!"

The chlorophyll giggles, saying, "I'm key!
I catch the rays while you sip your tea!
It's a recipe secret, I can't let out,
But plants get the perks, of that there's no doubt!"

The roots wiggle, like dancers in shoes,
"Make sure to share, we've paid our dues!
We hold you up when the wind blows wild,
Let's keep it fun, just like a child!"

So here's to the green, the laughter, the light,
In this botanical bash, everything feels right.
With each little sprout, the giggles arise,
Photosynthesis parties beneath the blue skies!

The Dance of Chlorophyll

In pots they sway, a leafy crew,
Doing their best to catch a view.
With roots that wiggle, they take the stage,
In this green ballet, they turn the page.

"More light!" they shout in photosynth song,
Giggling roots where they all belong.
Some do the twist, and others a spin,
Under the glow, let the party begin!

A fern in the back, with a frilly hat,
Tells the others, 'Let's chat and chat!'
While daisies gossip, with petals so bright,
They all laugh together, it's quite the sight!

So grab your soil, and let's plant a few,
Join the green dance, it's a leafy crew.
With stems so sturdy and leaves so spry,
The chlorophyll party is soaring high!

Beneath the Electric Sky

A bulb above, shining bright like the sun,
Leaves whisper secrets, oh what fun!
The violets giggle, the tomatoes hum,
As everyone here knows they're never glum.

With fluttering fronds and wiggle-waggle stems,
They joke on how sunlight gives life to their gems.
A cactus chimes in, 'I'm feeling so bold!'
'Don't take it too far, or I'll quietly scold!'

A potted spinach claims it's the star of the show,
While the herbs shake their leaves, saying, 'Oh no!'
In this electric haze, plants share their plight,
Dancing and jiving in the glow of the night.

Behind the glass, they wave and they cheer,
'Thanks to this light, we've conquered our fear!'
A garden of laughter, humor aflow,
Making the most of their luminous glow.

Threads of Green in Radiance

In a vibrant room, the leaves are alive,
With twists and twirls, they thrive and jive.
A minty fresh prince takes center stage,
As an odd little weed starts to dance with rage.

"Hey, I'm not just a pest," it shouts with delight,
"Watch me shimmy and shake in this dazzling light!"
A chorus of greens sings out loud and proud,
In this leafy cabaret, they are all so wowed.

A bromeliad bows, with flair in its pose,
Saying, "Watch me make photosynthesis glow!"
While ferns in the back create quite a scene,
With a jazz hand flourish, all wearing bright green.

"Let's twirl like the wind and sway with some grace,
We're more than just plants in this lovely space!"
Together they giggle, a cheerful brigade,
Spinning in joy, in this emerald parade!

The Garden of Ephemeral Light

A flash of green hops into the day,
As sprouts prance about, in the jazzy array.
"Who turned up the heat? It's quite a delight!"
Said the broad-leaved plant, feeling slightly uptight.

"Stay cool, my friends, we've still work to do,
More chlorophyll magic, with a wink and a coo!"
As daisies react with giggles and flair,
Choosing the dance-off for who gets the air.

A tiny herb shouts, "I'm the star of this show!"
With blossoms that quiver, puts on quite a show!
The kale claps its leaves, joins in for a spin,
In this fleeting glow, where the laughs begin.

So raise up your pots, and let's make some noise,
These plants know how to share their joys.
With each bright flash, green dreams take flight,
In the garden of laughter, bathed in warm light!

www.ingramcontent.com/pod-product-compliance
Lightning Source LLC
Chambersburg PA
CBHW072122070526
44585CB00016B/1532